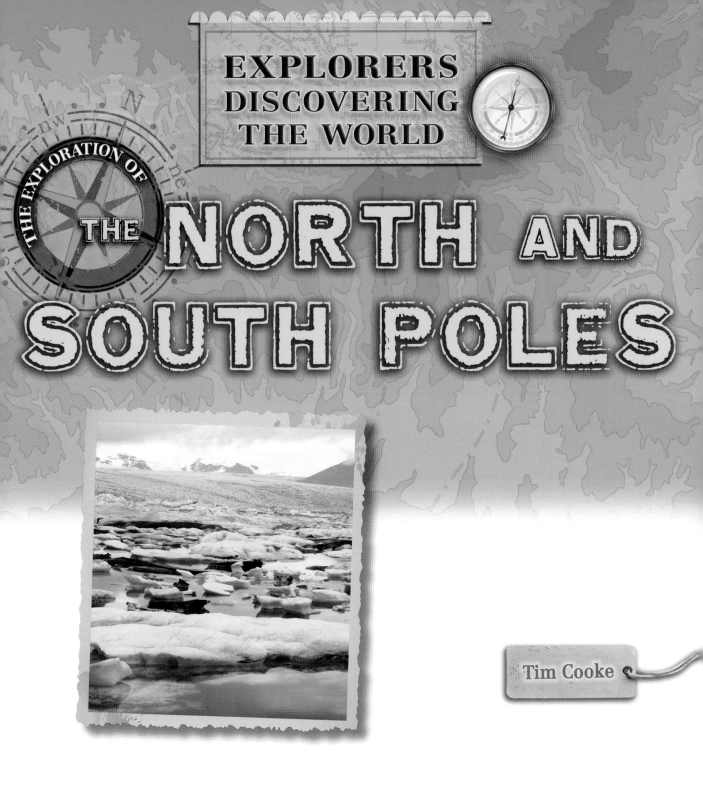

EXPLORERS DISCOVERING THE WORLD

THE EXPLORATION OF

THE NORTH AND SOUTH POLES

Tim Cooke

Gareth Stevens
Publishing

Please visit our website, www.garethstevens.com. For a free color catalog of all our high-quality books, call toll-free 1-800-542-2595 or fax 1-877-542-2596.

Library of Congress Cataloging-in-Publication Data

Cooke, Tim.
 The exploration of the north and south poles / Tim Cooke.
     p. cm. — (Explorers discovering the world)
 Includes index.
 ISBN 978-1-4339-8632-1 (pbk.)
 ISBN 978-1-4339-8633-8 (6-pack)
 ISBN 978-1-4339-8631-4 (library binding)
 1. North Pole—Discovery and exploration—Juvenile literature. 2. South Pole—Discovery and exploration—Juvenile literature. I. Title.
 G620.C66 2012
 910.911—dc23

                         2012039586

Published in 2013 by
Gareth Stevens Publishing
111 East 14th Street, Suite 349
New York, NY 10003

© 2013 Brown Bear Books Ltd

For Brown Bear Books Ltd:
Editorial Director: Lindsey Lowe
Managing Editor: Tim Cooke
Children's Publisher: Anne O'Daly
Art Director: Jeni Child
Designer: Lynne Lennon
Picture Manager: Sophie Mortimer

Picture Credits
Front Cover: Library of Congress: inset; **Thinkstock:** istockphoto main.

Clipart.com: 23b, 31, 38l; **Corbis:** Hulton Deutsch Collection 33; **istockphoto:** 11t, 11b; **Library of Congress:** 5t, 7b, 20, 23t, 28, 29, 37, 42, 43t, 44; **NASA:** 17; **National Archives:** National Science Foundation 32, 45; **Public Domain:** 7t, 16, 30, 41; **Robert Hunt Library:** 14l, 26r, 40, Bowdoin College 25, Hamburger Kunsthalle 10; **Shutterstock:** Antonio Abrignani 8, Christian Wilkinson 35, 38–39; **Thinkstock:** Design Pics, 15, 19, Digital Vision 9, Dorling Kindersley 43b, Hemera 6, istockphoto 5b, 22, 36, Photos.com 13, 14t, 27, 39; **Topfoto:** Topham Picturepoint 34, World History Archive 18:

Brown Bear Books has made every attempt to contact copyright holders. If anyone has any information please contact smortimer@windmillbooks.co.uk

Manufactured in the United States of America
1 2 3 4 5 6 7 8 9 12 11 10

CPSIA compliance information: Batch #CW13GS. For further information contact Gareth Stevens, New York, New York at 1-800-542-2595.

CONTENTS

INTRODUCTION

The polar regions were the last parts of the globe to be explored. The conditions inside the Arctic and the Antarctic Circles were some of the least hospitable on Earth. Inuit peoples lived around the fringes of the Arctic Ocean. On the great southern continent, Antarctica, even animals lived only near the coasts.

There was another reason the poles were so late to be explored. Much early exploration was fired by the desire to conquer land, increase trade, or spread religion. But after it became clear that any sea routes near the poles would be of limited value, there was only one reason left to go there: the thrill of exploration.

Race to the Poles

The first race came in the north, where explorers inched their way toward the pole. The first man with a real claim to have reached it was Robert Peary in 1909. Peary's claim sparked a new race, this time in the south. The contest ended in triumph for the Norwegian Roald Amundsen, but cost his competitors their lives.

Captain Robert F. Scott became a British hero for his brave attempt to reach the South Pole in 1912, when he and his companions died.

Ice floats on the Arctic Ocean: Until the 19th century, some people still believed there may be an open sea route to the North Pole.

EARLY ARCTIC EXPLORERS

By the late 1860s, much of the world had been mapped. The vast Arctic region, however, remained a mystery. In the 16th and 17th centuries, explorers such as Martin Frobisher and Henry Hudson had sailed northwest, but they had been forced to stop by barriers of ice.

DID YOU KNOW?

The Arctic is a frozen ocean. It contains more than 4 million square miles (almost 11 million sq km) of pack ice.

At the edges of the Arctic Ocean, ice drifts in blocks that often compact together to form what is known as pack ice.

THE INUIT

The Inuit are the native people of the Arctic Circle. Their lifestyle allows them to survive in a harsh environment that killed many explorers. The Inuit eat whales, fish, and seals, and live in igloos made from snow bricks or tents made from animal skins. They use dogs to pull sleds over the ice. They hunt caribou for meat and wear the fur to keep warm. Inuit skills may have helped explorers—but not all explorers asked the Inuit for their advice.

For centuries, the search for the Northwest Passage, a route around the top of North America, was defeated by ice. Within the Arctic Circle, even the ocean was frozen solid for the long winter months.

A Frozen Mystery

In the mid-19th century, a German scientist, Dr. August Petermann, suggsted that an ice-free sea existed at the North Pole. He argued that the Gulf Stream, a current of warm air from the tropics, kept the water from freezing. In May 1868, Petermann sent an expedition north to prove his point. The ship failed to find the open sea. So did later expeditions. Petermann was mistaken.

This Inuit woman and child were photographed in around 1900. The Inuit had learned how to keep warm by wearing layers of animal skin and fur.

JOHN ROSS

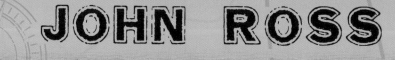

Arctic explorers had to be ready to become ice-bound and spend months in the ice; in Ross's case, the ship was stuck for four years.

In 1744, the British government had offered a £20,000 reward to whoever found the Northwest Passage. The Scottish naval officer John Ross sailed in 1818. He reached Lancaster Sound, north of Canada. The sound does lead to the Pacific, but Ross believed the way was blocked and turned back.

Ross's crew were dismayed. His decision was also criticized in London. Ross returned to the Arctic in 1829. For this voyage, he sailed in the *Victory*, a steam-powered paddle boat.

Trapped

This time, Ross sailed through the sound. He discovered the Boothia Peninsula, which he believed was the most northern point of North America. But *Victory* became trapped in the ice for the next four years. Eventually, the men traveled overland to Lancaster Sound. A passing whaling ship rescued them.

DID YOU KNOW?

Ross hoped that its steam engines would help *Victory* cut through the Arctic ice; in fact, it actually broke down frequently.

JAMES ROSS

James Ross, John Ross's nephew, accompanied his uncle on his Arctic expeditions. When the Victory *became icebound, James explored nearby land. In 1831, he became the first man to locate the magnetic North Pole, on the Boothia Peninsula. The pole is not the same as the North Pole. It marks where Earth's magnetic field points downward, and it's always moving. Ross also studied the lifestyles of the Inuit peoples of the region.*

The islands of the Arctic Ocean are frozen and often mountainous. They provided little shelter for crews while their boats were stuck in the ice.

1819–1827

WILLIAM PARRY

In 1824, the German artist Caspar David Friedrich painted The Sea of Ice, showing one of Parry's ships being destroyed by pack ice.

William Parry was second in command on John Ross's expedition in 1818. He did not support Ross's decision to abandon the expedition. Parry was given command of an Arctic expedition of his own in 1819. Its mission was to explore the north coast of America and to find the Northwest Passage.

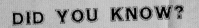

DID YOU KNOW?

During their winters in the Arctic Circle, Parry's crew passed the time organizing entertainment like comedy shows.

Parry sailed through Lancaster Sound, proving Ross was wrong to think it was an inlet. He discovered the Barrow Strait and a large island he named Melville Island, where they were frozen in for the winter.

More Expeditions

Between 1821 and 1825, Parry led three more expeditions to the Arctic. He sailed around Hudson Bay and spent the winters exploring on land. One of his crew found a whale skeleton on a cliff 100 feet (30 m) above sea level. Parry also studied the survival skills of the Inuit. In winter 1824, his ship became trapped in ice. Parry abandoned it and returned to England.

On a final expedition in 1827, William Parry set a record for traveling farthest north on the globe; his record stood for nearly 50 years.

SIR EDWARD SABINE

Sabine was a British astronomer who sailed to the Arctic with both John Ross and William Parry. He wanted to study Earth's magnetic field to work out the planet's shape. He later worked out that magnetic changes in Earth were linked to sunspots. Sabine's work led him to be asked to set up observatories around the world.

On Parry's 1824 expedition, naturalists studied the behavior of the polar bear, an animal that was only known about through a few exaggerated stories.

1818–1848

JOHN FRANKLIN

Sir John Franklin was a British naval officer who had already explored in Australia. In 1818, he tried to cross the Arctic Ocean from Norway to the Bering Strait. Ice forced him to give up. The next year, he joined William Parry's voyage to find the Northwest Passage. Franklin led the overland party that would explore the north coast of North America.

British explorers prepare for an expedition to the North Pole in 1880. Franklin helped open the way for British Arctic exploration for most of the 19th century.

This early 19th-century print shows two sailing ships towered over by walls of ice as they search for the Northwest Passage in stormy seas.

DID YOU KNOW?

On his trek from the Arctic coast to Great Slave Lake, Back ate lichen, some leather pants, and an old shoe to survive.

Franklin traveled north on the Coppermine River in what is now Canada until his party's canoes were damaged. Winter was setting in, and food was running out. An officer, George Back, trekked 1,200 miles (1,900 km) to get supplies.

Some Success

Franklin's second overland expedition of 1825–1827 succeeded in mapping much of the Arctic coast of mainland Canada. It was only in May 1845 that Franklin took command of a sailing expedition.

FUR TRADERS

Some of the earliest explorers in the frozen landscapes of northern Canada were fur traders. The pelts of animals like caribou and beaver were highly valuable. One of the most famous traders was Alexander Mackenzie, for whom the Mackenzie River is named. In 1789, he had followed the river from Great Slave Lake hoping it would lead to the Pacific. To his disappointment, it led to the Arctic Ocean.

Trapped in the ice, an explorer reads to his companions. Along with the harsh conditions, boredom was one of the worst enemies faced by polar explorers.

This note, written by the captains of the two ships, finally explained Franklin's death and the fate of the rest of the party; it was not discovered until 1859.

Franklin's two ships, the *Erebus* and the *Terror*, were to sail through the Canadian Arctic archipelago. Then they were to use the Northwest Passage to get to the Bering Strait.

Franklin Disappears

By late July 1845, Franklin's two ships had reached Baffin Bay, west of Greenland. They were seen there by a whaling ship. That was the last sighting of the expedition. Because Arctic expeditions became stuck in the ice and lasted a long time, no one missed Franklin for over a year. But meanwhile, the expedition had run into disaster.

No Survivors

Disaster struck when the two ships got stuck in ice near King William Island. Twenty-three officers and men died from starvation and scurvy, including Franklin himself. In April 1848, his second in command, Francis Crozier, ordered the ships to be abandoned. He set out on foot to lead the survivors to the mouth of the Back River in Canada, but they all died. Crozier left notes explaining the fate of the expedition. But who would ever read them?

DID YOU KNOW?

Francis Crozier visited the Arctic with William Parry in 1821 and returned three years later on Parry's third expedition.

GEORGE BACK

George Back accompanied Franklin on three Arctic expeditions. In 1833, Back led his own expedition to find John Ross, who was missing. When he learned that Ross was safe, Back decided to explore the Great Slave Lake area. The Back River is named for him. Back explored much of the northern Canadian coastline on that and a later trip.

This hut on an island at the entrance to the Northwest Passage was built by Franklin to store supplies for the journey home—but no explorers came back.

THE SEARCH FOR FRANKLIN

After John Franklin had been missing for three years, the British Admiralty sent an expedition to the Arctic to look for him. It was the first of many over the next decade. These expeditions also continued to explore: among their achievements was the final discovery of the Northwest Passage.

The hunt for Franklin or clues to his fate drew British explorers to the wastes of the Arctic for many decades after he died.

DID YOU KNOW?

In 1852, Lady Jane Franklin funded an expedition to find her husband; she offered a large reward for his rescue.

This satellite image of James Ross Strait shows how forbidding and bleak the winter landscape of the Arctic can be.

The first man sent to the Arctic was James Ross. Ross had actually been intended to lead Franklin's ill-fated expedition, but he had been replaced by Franklin. Ross reached Peel Sound, south of King William Island, where Franklin's ships had been stuck in the ice. He was forced to turn back just 70 miles (110 km) short of the wrecks of the *Erebus* and the *Terror*.

Franklin Was Here

The British government and private individuals launched more expeditions to find Franklin, but with no success. In 1850, Richard Collinson sailing on the *Enterprise* and Robert McClure on the *Investigator* decided to sail from the northern Pacific to the Arctic to look for Franklin.

LADY FRANKLIN

Lady Jane married John Franklin in 1828. She joined him on his foreign posts. When they lived in Tasmania, she traveled to Australia and New Zealand. She continued to travel around the world after her husband's death was proved. She visited Japan and the American West. She became the first woman to receive the Gold Medal of the English Royal Geographical Society, in 1857.

This illustration shows Robert McClure, discoverer of the Northwest Passage, meeting men from a Royal Navy ship during his explorations.

Collinson spent the winters from 1851 to 1853 on Victoria Island. Some Inuit gave him what may have been an engine from one of Franklin's ships. No one with Collinson could speak Inuit, however, so they could not find out more.

The Northwest Passage

Meanwhile, McClure explored overland. In October 1850, he found Melville Island and realized that it marked the western exit of the Northwest Passage. On the north coast, he found an open channel, which is named in his honor.

DID YOU KNOW?

Frederick Schwatka led an expedition to King William Island in 1878. It was the last voyage in search of Franklin.

The Mystery Is Solved

In April 1854, the Scottish explorer John Rae met Inuit on the Boothia Peninsula. They said some white men had died and showed Rae some of Franklin's possessions. The British Admiralty concluded that Franklin was dead. Franklin's wife, Lady Jane, asked Francis McClintock to search again. On King William Island, McClintock found more evidence of the expedition: the bodies of British seamen and the expedition log.

WHAT HAPPENED?

Francis McClintock found the log of Franklin's expedition hidden in a tin on King William Island in Victoria Strait. The log showed that the ships had sailed west through Lancaster Sound before ice stopped them. As they tried to escape, Franklin's crew all died from starvation, scurvy, or the cold. Franklin himself died on April 24, 1848.

Later explorers found many preserved signs of Franklin's expedition, like this marker in Nunavut in northern Canada.

1860–1871

CHARLES HALL

As a boy, the American Charles Hall was fascinated by John Franklin's disappearance in the Arctic. He later managed to raise money for an expedition to look for the explorer. By then, it was 15 years since Franklin's voyage. Hall argued that, if any of Franklin's party had adopted the Inuit way of life, they might have survived.

During his Arctic explorations, Charles Hall made accurate maps of the coast of Greenland, as well as reaching the farthest point north of anyone.

DID YOU KNOW?

Hall learned to live like an Inuit. He wore furs and skins, lived in an igloo, ate raw seal, and traveled with a sled and dogs.

After Hall's death, his expedition was shipwrecked; they survived by floating on ice for six months until they reached land.

On his first trip to the Arctic in 1860, Hall found remains of Martin Frobisher's 16th-century visit. Hall returned home to raise funds for a second expedition, but this was delayed by the start of the Civil War in 1861.

The Far North

Hall returned to the Arctic in 1864. He lived for five years with Inuit, who told him what had happened to Franklin's party. In 1871, he returned once more to the Arctic. He traveled farther north than anyone before him, reaching latitude 82° 11' N. But Hall died of heart failure during the return trip.

GEORGE NARES

Briton George Nares was a skilled sailor. In 1875, he led an expedition up the west coast of Greenland. He was inexperienced in Arctic conditions and his crew soon suffered from exhaustion and scurvy. But Nares did return safely, having proved that Greenland was an island. He also proved that the Arctic Ocean was permanently frozen. There was no open water route to the North Pole.

FRIDTJOF NANSEN

Nansen's plan to deliberately get stuck in the ice was based on the fact that the ice slowly moves as it floats on the surface of the Arctic Ocean.

Norwegian zoologist Fridtjof Nansen was fascinated by the Inuit and had crossed Greenland on skis. He came up with a crazy plan to build a ship that was strong enough to withstand sea ice. He would sail into the Arctic Ocean then, when the ocean froze, let the ice move him toward the North Pole.

Nansen's lecture tours about his trip to the Arctic made him one of the most famous personalities in Europe at the end of the 19th century.

Nansen left Oslo in 1893 on board *Fram*. The ship was soon locked in the Arctic ice. For a year, it slowly drifted north.

A Remarkable Achievement

Nansen became impatient, and in March 1895, he left the ship to head for the pole by dog sled. *Fram*, meanwhile, drifted to Spitsbergen, where it broke free from the ice. Nansen and a companion made it to within 240 miles (385 km) of the pole before they began the long trek home. *Fram* sailed back to Norway.

NILS NORDENSKJÖLD

Baron Nils Nordenskjöld was a Swedish scientist who was obsessed with the Arctic. He first traveled to Spitsbergen in 1858. He spent the next 20 years exploring Greenland. He even tried to get to the North Pole using reindeer to pull his sleds. His biggest contribution to Arctic exploration was to prove that it was possible to navigate through the Northeast Passage around the top of Siberia.

When Fram sailed back to Christiana, its home port in Norway, in September 1895, it was greeted by the largest crowds the city had ever seen.

ROBERT E. PEARY

Pennsylvanian Robert Edwin Peary is one of America's most famous Arctic explorers—but also one of the most controversial. Peary claimed to be the first man to reach the North Pole, on April 6, 1909. But many people at the time doubted his claim, and experts are still divided about it.

A team of husky dogs pulls a sled over the ice. Huskies are specially adapted to live in the bitter cold of the Arctic winter.

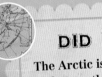

DID YOU KNOW?

The Arctic is an unstable mass of ice and snow that forms in piles and drifts, making it hard to cross on foot.

Robert E. Peary was driven by his ambition to be the first man to reach the North Pole—but did his ambition tempt him to make inaccurate claims?

Peary was determined to do something during his lifetime for which he would be remembered. He studied engineering before joining the U.S. Navy in 1881. When he read Nils Nordenskjöld's accounts of his polar exploration, he decided that he would become the first man to reach the North Pole.

Planning for the Pole

In 1886, aged 30, Peary tried to cross Greenland but failed. When he tried again five years later, he broke his leg. As he recovered, he studied the survival techniques of the Inuit. Anxious that others might reach the pole first, such as the Norwegian Otto Sverdrup, Peary set about raising funds for an expedition.

SLEDS AND DOGS

One of the keys to Peary's success was his use of dog sleds to travel over the ice. Inuit in Greenland and Siberia had long used husky dogs to pull their sleds. Unlike ponies, dogs can tolerate the conditions. But dogs can be a bit crazy, so they need a good driver to control them. Sleds changed over time. The Inuit used frozen fish instead of wood for runners: the fish were more pliable than the wood, so they passed more smoothly over the rough ice surface.

1886–1909

These drawings tell the story of Peary's servant Matthew Henson; the African American helped Peary to communicate with the Inuit.

...ED AS AN ARCTIC EXPLORER, ...REER IN THE JUNGLES OF ...RICA! — PEARY, SO IMPRESSED ...HENSON'S ABILITY, KEPT HIM AS ...T ON ALL HIS SUBSEQUENT

MAT HENSON
ONLY LIVING AMERICAN TO SET FOOT ON THE NORTH POLE.

HENSON'S GREAT KNOW-LEDGE OF ESKIMO LIFE AND LANGUAGE, AND HIS ENGAGING PERSONALITY, MADE HIM THE MOST IN-DISPENSABLE MEMBER OF THE EXPEDITION. — FOR THE FINAL DASH TO THE POLE, PEARY CHOSE FIVE MEN — FOUR ESKIMOS AND MAT HENSON!

ACCORDING TO COMMANDER MACMILLAN, IT WAS HENSON WHO ACTUALLY PLANTED THE STARS AND STRIPES ON TOP OF THE WORLD, W... EXHAUSTED AND ILL, SAT ON THE SLEDGE AND F... HIS HAND

The Peary Arctic Club raised money to buy a ship, the *Theodore Roosevelt*, that could break through ice. Peary began his voyage in 1905, already 50 years old. But although he had spent years preparing for his trip and used Inuit guides, Peary was defeated by temperatures as low as –60°F (–51°C).

At what he claimed was the North Pole, Peary had the party photographed with a number of flags, including the Stars and Stripes.

Another Attempt

In July 1908, he set off again. In Greenland, he recruited 50 Inuit and 250 dogs. An overland party set off in February 1909.

By April 1, Peary was just 150 miles (240 km) from the pole. He sent some of the party back to the ship. They included the group's most experienced navigator.

Pole or Not?

Peary went on with his servant, Matt Henson, and four Inuit. He claimed to reach the pole on April 6. That would mean the men covered the last part of the journey in 30 miles (48 km) a day. Was that possible?

FREDERICK COOK

One person to doubt Peary's claim to be the first man to reach the North Pole was Frederick Cook. The Brooklyn-born explorer claimed to have reached the pole a year earlier, on April 21, 1908. In February 1908, Cook left Annoatok in northern Greenland; he returned 14 months later. His claim to have reached the pole was believed at first until Peary denounced Cook as a liar. Cook never produced any navigational records to prove his claim.

This French cartoon shows the American explorers Peary and Cook fighting over their claim to be the first to the North Pole.

1897–1955

AIR EXPLORATION

Byrd's successful flight over the North Pole used a Fokker monoplane, like this one being used on an expedition to the Antarctic in 1929.

The late 19th and early 20th centuries saw the birth of aviation. Soon Arctic explorers took to the skies. The Swede Salomon Andrée tried to reach the North Pole by air balloon in 1897. The balloon disappeared, together with Andrée and his companions. In 1926, American Richard E. Byrd became the first man to fly over the pole in a small monoplane.

In 1926, the Norwegian polar explorer Roald Amundsen reached the North Pole on the airship *Norge*, designed by the Italian Umberto Nobile. But the two men fell out over who should take credit for the success.

The Fate of the Italia

Nobile's next airship, the *Italia*, crashed on its way back from the North Pole in May 1928. Amundsen flew to help look for his enemy. He died when his seaplane crashed.

DID YOU KNOW?

Byrd's average speed was 90 miles per hour (144 km/h). The top speed of Peary's dog sleds was 30 mph (48 km/h).

The giant airship Norge *is towed from its hangar ready for Amundsen and Nobile to set out for the pole in 1926.*

LOUISE BOYD

A glamorous and wealthy heiress from California, Boyd became the first woman to fly over the North Pole in 1955. She was then 68 years old. Earlier in her life, she had used much of her fortune to pay for Arctic expeditions, many of which she undertook with her friends. Boyd had even joined the search for Amundsen in 1928, when his seaplane crashed.

NI

NORGE

EARLY ANTARCTIC EXPLORATION

By the early 20th century, there was only one vast continent that had not been explored by humans: Antarctica. Unlike the Arctic, Antarctica has no native people. In fact, no land mammals live there at all. Only penguins, whales, and seals survive in the unforgiving conditions around its coasts.

On Ross Island, just off the Antarctic coast, pressure has pushed up the ice into jagged ridges that make traveling overland very difficult.

DID YOU KNOW?

The Antarctic covers around 5 million square miles (over 13 million sq km). All of it is frozen all year around.

Whirling snow falls past an iceberg during an Antarctic blizzard. The continent is the least hospitable place on Earth.

British sailor Captain James Cook explored Antarctic waters in the 1770s. Cook noted the huge numbers of seals and whales. Whaling ships were soon visiting the region. Another visitor was Sir John Ross. In the 1840s, 10 years after he had found the magnetic North Pole, he sailed to Antarctica looking for the magnetic South Pole.

Land Exploration

The first exploration of Antarctica was made by Carl Larsen, a Norwegian whaler captain, in 1893. After raising money for another expedition, he left Melbourne, Australia, on board the *Antarctic* in 1894.

TERRIBLE WINTER

The North and the South Poles have less sunshine than anywhere else in the world, but the South Pole gets even less than the North Pole. This means that Antarctica has the worst winter in the world. The sun disappears completely between May and August. Hurricane-force winds blow for days at a time. Low-pressure systems in the southern seas keep the air freezing. Temperatures fall as low as –128.6°F (–89.2°C). That can kill humans. The British explorer Robert Falcon Scott wrote in his diary, "Great God! this is an awful place."

Cotton Glacier in western Antarctica is 10 miles (16 km) long and flows into the Southern Ocean.

Larsen's expedition included Carsten Borchgrevink, a Norwegian scientist who lived in Australia. He explored some of the Antarctic continent.

Carsten Borchgrevink

Borchgrevink organized his own expedition. He asked a British magazine to sponsor him to be the first man to spend a winter on mainland Antarctica. Borchgrevink sailed from London in August 1898. In February, having pushed through the ice, he reached the coast and found a place to land.

DID YOU KNOW?

Borchgrevink climbed to the summit of Cape Adare before the winter set in. Its peak is 3,670 feet (1,100 m) high.

Harsh Winter

When the freezing winter came, the whole expedition was confined to its hut for 75 days. But only one man died. That suggested Antarctica was not as inhospitable as people had feared. When the ship returned to collect the explorers, it sailed along the coast while Borchgrevink and a dog handler sledded south. They reached latitude 78° 50' S, further south than anybody had ever been. The Royal Geographical Society in London had predicted that Borchgrevink would fail. When he returned to England in 1900, it had to acknowledge his achievement.

Whalers pose on top of a whale they have dragged onto an island in the Antarctic, ready to cut it up for meat and blubber.

WHALERS

Some of the first seafarers in Antarctic waters were whalers from northern Europe. Since the 11th century, whales had been hunted for their meat and blubber, or fat. Before electric lighting, blubber was boiled down to produce oil for lamps. The sperm whale's oil was used in cosmetics and candles. In the early 20th century, Norway dominated the whale trade—and polar exploration.

THE BELGICA

The *Belgica* was a former Norwegian whale-hunting ship. In 1897, it left Belgium for the Antarctic with the U.S. explorer Frederick Cook and the Norwegian Roald Amundsen. The Belgian naval officer Adrien de Gerlache led the expedition.

After its adventures in Antarctica, the Belgica was used in an expedition to the Arctic before returning to whaling.

Ice from glaciers slides into the sea, where it helps form pack ice around the Antarctic coast.

It took five months to reach the Antarctic Circle. In January 1898, de Gerlache and his men landed on the Antarctic mainland.

A Harsh Winter

The Antarctic weather was surprisingly mild, so de Gerlache decided to explore further south. He assumed the Antarctic winter would be warmer than the Arctic winter. He was wrong. Before long, the boat became trapped by frozen ice. For the next 347 days, the men were trapped, despite their efforts to escape.

DID YOU KNOW?

The *Belgica*'s crew was badly suited for the Antarctic. Many men had heart and digestive problems, or bad circulation.

ESCAPING THE ICE

Summer reached Antarctica in November. The Belgica's crew was desperate to escape before winter returned. They tried to blow a path through the ice using explosives, but only managed to dent the ice. As fall arrived, they tried one last thing. They would saw through the ice. It took two and a half months of hard work before the ship was freed. On March 28, 1899, they escaped.

1902–1903

OTTO NORDENSKJÖLD

Otto Nordenskjöld was the nephew of Nils Nordenskjöld, the Swedish Arctic explorer. In February 1902, Otto and five companions landed on Snow Hill Island in Antarctica. They spent a year exploring with dog teams and found evidence of life over 100 million years old. In February 1903, they returned to the coast—but their ship did not turn up.

A seal rests on ice on the Antarctic coast. Seal meat helped keep Nordenskjöld and his companions alive during the long polar winter.

LUCKY RESCUE

The ship that rescued Nordenskjöld was the Argentine naval vessel Uruguay. *On what was planned as the ship's last night in the Antarctic, its dogs started to bark. They had sensed men on land. The* Uruguay *rescued the crew of Nordenskjöld's ship, the* Antarctic. *Now luck also brought them to Nordenskjöld and his companions. The whole crew of the* Antarctic *had been rescued.*

The men were forced to kill seals and penguins for food. There was still no sign of rescue as their second winter began.

Hope at Last!

On October 12, 1903, the men spotted two dark shapes that they thought were penguins. They turned out to be sailors from the rescue ship, looking for Nordenskjöld. They, too, had been stranded in Antarctica all winter. All the men now waited for rescue. But when a ship appeared on November 8, it was not the one they expected.

DID YOU KNOW?

Frenchman Jean-Baptiste Charcot came to Antarctica to rescue Nordenskjöld but spent five years charting the coastline.

ERNEST SHACKLETON

The Irish sailor Ernest Shackleton loved adventure. He accompanied the British explorer Robert Scott on his expedition to Antarctica in 1904. But Shackleton became so sick from scurvy that Scott sent him home. That did not stop Shackleton from making another expedition.

On his first voyage to the Antarctic, Shackleton's remarkable strength and courage could not prevent him from becoming very sick from scurvy.

DID YOU KNOW?

Much of Antarctica is mountainous; it lies at an elevation of over 9,500 feet (2,900 m) above sea level.

Shackleton was a good friend and colleague of the British polar explorer Robert Falcon Scott, who made his own bid for the South Pole in 1912.

In 1907, Shackleton advertised in a newspaper for volunteers for an expedition to the South Pole. His ship was a Norwegian sealing vessel, the *Nimrod*. He took Siberian ponies rather than troublesome sled dogs.

Antarctica!

By October 1908, Shackleton's crew had set up food stores on the Antarctic mainland ready for an attempt to reach the magnetic and geographic poles. Shackleton and three companions set off for the geographic South Pole on November 6.

On Shackleton's 1914 expedition, 22 men from the Endurance survived for four and a half months on Elephant Island while Shackleton went for help.

POLAR EQUIPMENT

Shackleton packed well for his expedition. He used reindeer-skin sleeping bags that were big enough for three men to sleep together to keep warm. He ordered special boots from Lapland made from reindeer skin. His sleds came from Norway. The ski equipment and mittens were made of wolf and dog skin.

The men were walking into the unknown. Before long, one of the ponies became too weak to continue. The men killed and ate it. In less than three weeks, they had passed the furthest point south that Scott had reached in 1904, but they only had three ponies left to carry their supplies.

A Slow Climb

Within a week, only one pony remained, but the men were making good progress. They were thousands of feet above sea level. Then the last pony fell into a crevasse, taking food supplies.

The Nimrod *was Shackleton's ship for the polar expedition in 1908. Most of the crew spent the winter on the ship, stuck in the ice, as they waited for Shackleton to return.*

When they reached South Georgia, the men used the James Caird, shown here, as a sledge to slide down icy slopes.

On Christmas Day 1908, Shackleton and his men stood on the glacier that leads to the central Antarctic plateau. They were just 250 miles (400 km) from the South Pole. But with no ponies left, they were pulling their sleds themselves.

A Near Miss

By January 9, 1909, the men were at an altitude of 11,000 feet (3,350 m). They were running out of food. They suffered terrible headaches because of the high altitude and the brightness of the snow. Shackleton decided they could go no further. Reluctantly, they headed for home.

THE *JAMES CAIRD*

In 1914, Shackleton set out to become the first man to cross Antarctica overland. But when his ship was smashed in the ice, the crew took to their open whaling boats. They drifted to Elephant Island. Shackleton and five others sailed one of the boats, James Caird, to South Georgia for help. The 800-mile (1,300 km) journey crossed rough seas, but the men made it in under three weeks.

RACE FOR THE SOUTH POLE

Captain Scott and his companions reached the South Pole to find they had lost the race to get there first. All five men died on the return journey.

The race to reach the South Pole came down to an Englishman and a Norwegian. Robert Falcon Scott and Roald Amundsen both had experience of polar travel. Scott had tried to reach the South Pole in 1904. Amundsen was on his way to the North Pole when he learned Robert E. Peary had got there first.

Amundsen sailed south on the *Fram*, the former ship of polar explorer Fridtjof Nansen. Scott sailed from London and reached Melbourne, Australia, in October, 1910. There, he learned that Amundsen was planning to race him to the South Pole.

Roald Amundsen was the most successful of the polar explorers and achieved many "firsts" in both the north and the south.

Different Preparations

Amundsen had prepared well. He brought 97 dogs from Greenland and just 19 men. They were traveling light. Scott, on the other hand, was weighed down with equipment, men, ponies, and caterpillar-tracked motor vehicles.

Amundsen and his men spent three days making sure that they had made their calculations correctly and had actually reached the South Pole.

ROALD AMUNDSEN

Norwegian Roald Amundsen was obsessed with the poles. He was on the first expedition to Antarctica and was the first man to cross the Northwest Passage. He also crossed the Northeast Passage. He was the first man to reach the South Pole and the first to undisputedly reach the North Pole (1926). He disappeared in the Arctic in June 1928.

DID YOU KNOW?

In 1910, Amundsen sent Scott a telegram that read, "Beg leave to inform you proceeding Antarctica."

It was soon clear that Scott had made a mistake. The ponies could not cope with the weather, and the vehicles broke down. In contrast, Amundsen's dogs performed well. They pulled the sleds up onto the central Antarctic plateau.

The Pole

Amundsen was soon far ahead of Scott and passed the furthest point Shackleton had reached. On December 14, 1911, the Norwegians' instruments told them they were at the South Pole. At 3:00 P.M., they planted the Norwegian flag. They then spent three days checking their readings.

Captain Robert Falcon Scott updates his diary in the hut he built in the Antarctic as the base for his expedition to the South Pole.

DID YOU KNOW?

Amundsen was not sure where the South Pole was, so his men covered a larger area that they knew must contain it.

The Southern Lights, caused by electrical activity, light up the sky above the Amundsen–Scott South Pole Station.

Scott, meanwhile, realized his expedition was in trouble. About 170 miles (270 km) from the South Pole, he sent the support party back. He went on with just four men.

A Disastrous End

As they got closer to the pole, the men saw Amundsen's tracks in the snow. They realized the Norwegian had reached the pole first. The British explorers reached the pole a month after Amundsen. They camped overnight and then started the painful journey back. They never made it. All five men died of cold and starvation. Their courage made them heroes in Britain.

THE POLE TODAY

The South Pole today is as inhospitable as it was in 1911, but it is now home to a research station. The United States built the Amundsen–Scott South Pole Station in 1956 and named it for the first two men to reach the South Pole. Scientists live there year-round. All the world's nations own Antarctica. The scientists work in a spirit of cooperation.

airship An aircraft with a balloon of gas that is driven by a motor.

altitude The height of something above sea level.

Arctic Circle An imaginary circle drawn around the globe at a latitude of 66° 33' north of the Equator.

blubber Fat from sea mammals used to make oil for fuel.

caribou A wild reindeer from North America.

continent A very large landmass.

crevasse A deep crack in a glacier.

expedition A journey made for a particular purpose.

glacier A large, thick sheet of ice that slips down a slope into the sea.

husky A powerful dog with thick fur that is traditionally used to pull sleds in the Arctic.

igloo A domed shelter built by the Inuit using bricks cut from ice or packed snow.

latitude The position of a location on Earth's surface either north or south relative to the equator.

log A careful record of a journey or expedition.

pack ice A crust of ice that forms on the surface of the ocean.

peninsula A narrow piece of land that juts into water.

plateau A high, flat area among mountains or hills.

scurvy A serious disease caused by lack of vitamin C.

sled A vehicle on runners that can be pulled or pushed over snow or ice.

sound A narrow stretch of water that connects two larger bodies of water.

FURTHER INFORMATION

Books

Anderson, Harry S. *Exploring the Polar Regions* (Discovery and Exploration). Chelsea House Publications, 2009.

Johnson, Kristen. *The* Endurance *Expedition*. Essential Library, 2011.

Knudsen, Anders. *Sir John Franklin: The Search for the Northwest Passage* (In the Footsteps of Explorers). Crabtree Publishing Company, 2010.

Nardo, Dan. *Polar Expeditions* (World History). Lucent Books, 2011.

Sherman, Josepha. *Exploring the North Pole: The Story of Robert Edwin Peary and Matthew Henson* (Monumental Milestones). Mitchell Lane Publishers, 2005.

Shone, Rob, and Nick Spender. *Defying Death at the North and South Poles* (Graphic Survival Stories). Rosen Central, 2010.

Websites

http://www.freezeframe.ac.uk/ home/home
Scott Polar Research Institute archive of images of polar research from 1845 to 1982.

http://www.rmg.co.uk/scott
Royal Museums Greenwich pages

about British explorer Captain Robert Falcon Scott.

http://polardiscovery.whoi.edu/ index.html
Woods Hole Oceanographic Institution pages on polar discovery, including timelines of exploration.